Talking
It Over

Just
The Two
Of Us

# Nick and Joan Murray

Talking
It Over

Just
The Two
Of Us

**A GUIDE FOR THE
FINANCIAL ADVISOR'S
LIFE PARTNER**

"

We dedicate this book
to our children,
and to theirs.

# Contents

# 1

# Why We Are Writing This Book

# Nick

"

The finest, noblest work one can do in this world is to advise people about how they can secure their financial futures. It isn't a job, or even a career. It's a calling. I believed that, however indistinctly, when I entered the profession nearly half a century ago. I believe it infinitely more strongly and clearly today.

And sound financial advice is desperately needed by the people around us. We live in the most successful economy in history, yet it's not too much to say that ours is a nation of financial illiterates, because the fundamentals of personal finance are all but untaught in our schools.

Moreover, most of the day-to-day financial pressure people feel—as well as nearly all the peer pressure—is to consume rather than to save: to meet today's immediate needs and wants rather than to provide for tomorrow's.

That's why the financial advisor was sent into the world.

To understand and appreciate this profession, there are two critically important things you need to know. First is that there is no limit to the good that we advisors can do, nor to how long that good—passing down the generations—may go on. And the corollary is that there's no limit to the money we can earn doing that good. Indeed, the iron law of the financial advisor's compensation is that the more good we do, the more we earn.

This pretty much concludes the good news.

There is no bad news; there's only the reality of the business, which is challenging enough. It's simply that, unlike a physician who is sought out by patients who sense that they're ill, the financial advisor builds a business by offering help to people who have not asked for it. We are like doctors who go from door to door making house calls on people who (a) don't

> **There is no limit to the good that we advisors can do, nor to how long that good—passing down the generations—may go on.**

know they're sick, (b) know they're sick but refuse to admit it, (c) know they're sick but don't trust us to help, (d) know they're sick but don't really want to get better, (e) are hoping to find a cheaper doctor, or (f) just refuse to talk about this with some stranger who came and knocked on their door unbidden.

Let me reduce the foregoing paragraph to one sentence: *for a very long time, almost everyone we prospect with the offer of our genuinely priceless help will say no.*

This can be a psychologically devastating experience. And for most people who enter the financial services industry, it's an experience that ultimately defeats them. So much so that, at the end of the fifth year in personal production, as many as four out of five financial advisors will have left the business. They simply cannot go on. "No"—the seemingly ceaseless, relentless onslaught of "no"— just hurts too much.

In my time, I came as close as to succumbing to "no" as it is possible to come without actually slipping into the darkness. And I believe I would probably have flunked out of the business—as I've said in my prospecting book *The Game of Numbers*, and lots of other places—had it not been for the faith, courage and determination of my wife, Joan.

# Joan

No, he wouldn't have, though it's nice of Nick to say so. We'll never know, but it's certainly true that we succeeded—that is, he first of all failed to fail—because of the true partnership that we evolved.

That's why we're writing this book. Because if the training that advisors receive is powerless to keep four out of five people in the profession until they succeed, then their life partners—their significant others—

obviously get no training *at all*. Heaven knows we want to help, but are given not the slightest clue as to how to go about it.

This is just a human tragedy, because the most basic truism in all relationships is that two heads are better than one. In fact, our personal experience goes far beyond that truth. It suggests that two minds, working in harmony toward a common goal, are far more powerful than either of the two minds, *and indeed are vastly stronger and more creative than the sum of the two minds.*

We can't really tell you why this works, much less how. We can only promise you that it does.

We don't have any formal training in this. We're not marriage counselors—talk about the blind leading the blind! He's not Ozzie, and I'm not Harriet. We don't do couples therapy, much less family therapy.

Nor is this book in any way just for
"husbands" and "wives." (To the extent
that it may speak to a husband and a wife,
we never assume which one is the advisor.)
We're not being at all gender specific, regardless of which pronoun we're using at
any given moment. Our audience is any and
every committed relationship/domestic partnership in which one of the parties is building a financial services career.

We're writing this book, finally, because there
doesn't seem to be any other book on this
subject. And our only qualifications for doing
so are, first of all, that since Nick has been in
the business for 45 years, and I've been with
him every step of the way, we have a total of
90 person-years of experience to offer you.
And second, that experience has certainly
worked for us. We're sure it can work for you
as well—*provided that the both of you
really want it to.*

Let me begin with our story.

# 2

# How It All Started

# Joan

"

So there I am. It's 1969; I'm 25 years old, with a newborn daughter, and I've given up my own Wall Street career to rear her and the other children to come.

(That was always the plan. When Nick and I were first dating—a verb which in those days didn't mean to two Catholic school kids what it means now—I asked him what he wanted out of life. He blurted out, "A house full of kids and dogs." And I went: Bingo.)

My husband is the same age as I, and he's in his second year as a stockbroker on commission, which means he cold-calls total strangers all day long and offers to manage their investment portfolios. This is something we both know he is not really qualified to do, because there is no money at all,

> *I always say when you're at your wits' end, with no idea where to turn, go clean out a closet.*

much less any investment experience, in either of our backgrounds.

He's very enthusiastic, but perhaps not terribly credible, and most everyone he approaches is saying no. Intellectually, we know that this is what he signed up for— and was indeed well trained to expect—but it has begun to wear him down emotionally.

Moreover, a major bear market in stocks has just gotten underway, and the people who *do* buy stocks from Nick are piling up losses. Since all he ever wanted to do was to make money for people while doing the same for us, letting his clients down (as he perceives it) hurts even worse than "no."

Suffice it to say that our income is nowhere near what we had hoped it would be, nor even where we need it to be. (Let it go at that, if you will. But just know this: *you do not have it any harder than I did in those first bitter years.*) We are in a very tough spot, and it's getting tougher by the day.

So what do I do? Well, I always say when you're at your wits' end, with no idea where to turn, go clean out a closet. It was and remains some kind of occupational therapy to me.

There's a stack of books at the top of the closet. Nick brought them home from his training class, but I've never seen him read them. And as I'm trying to move them, with the baby in my other arm, one book falls out, right on my head. I pick it up, and I see it's called ***Think and Grow Rich*** by Napoleon Hill. I still couldn't tell you why, but I sit down and start reading it. And I'm still reading it when my husband comes home.

All I can think to say to him is, "Is this book true?"

# Nick

"

My answer, of course, is that I don't know; I've never read it. So we put the baby to bed, sit down, and start reading it *together.*

(That turns out to be the key, although we don't realize it at the time. If Joan had said, "You ought to read this and see what you think," I'm sure that, even if I *had* read it— which still seems doubtful—it wouldn't have had anywhere near the same effect.)

We read: every adversity carries with it the seed of an equivalent or greater benefit.

We read: whatever the mind of man can conceive and believe, it can achieve.

We read: you have to shut out all negative influences—including (and especially) the

**We're totally and irrevocably in business together. We're equal partners, albeit with different duties.**

"advice" of family members and well-meaning "friends," subtly implying that you ought to give up and get a real job.

We read: two minds working in harmony on a purpose and a plan to which they both wholeheartedly commit somehow plug into an intelligence greater than either or both of them.

And we're hooked.

We're totally and irrevocably in business together. We're equal partners, albeit with different duties. We're going to work on that partnership every day. And the possibility of failure has ceased to exist.

Is that what you and your partner really want? And are you prepared to pay the price?

# 3

# Do You Really Want To Be A Partner?

# Joan

"

Being the life partner of a person working—
and perhaps, in the early years, struggling —to
build a successful financial advice practice is
not a spectator sport, and it's not for the faint
of heart. It may at times put a strain on your
ability to get your own needs met. You have
to really want to share in, and to be a
positive influence on, that struggle.

And believe me, you already have a

partnership agreement in force. Neither of you may be conscious of its terms and provisions, but by the sheer act of living with an advisor, the two of you have reached some kind of accommodation.

He goes out the door in the morning, and you say, "Have a great day." He comes home at night, and you say, "How was your day?" (And some evenings you're only half listening to the answer, because you have your own very real career challenges and/or because the toddler is just now gleefully pulling all the household chemicals out from under the sink.)

Well, don't look now, but there's your partner-ship agreement. The two of you never wrote it out and signed it. You never even sat down and agreed on it verbally. You just kind of defaulted to it. It's totally unhelpful at best—why not just come right out and say, "Kiddo, you're on your own"—and a ticking time bomb at worst. It can't possibly be what either of you really wants. *But it is the agreement you've both made.*

Time to make a new agreement—a real one this time.

Real in the sense that you've talked it through and consciously agreed on it. *Real in the sense that you've written it out and signed it.* (If it isn't written, it isn't real.) And real in the

**"**

*Believe me, you already have a partnership agreement in force. Neither of you may be conscious of its terms and provisions, but by the sheer act of living with an advisor, the two of you have reached some kind of accommodation.*

sense that you re-read it together, and re-commit to it, every day.

It can start as simply as a daily statement: in the morning, of what your partner proposes to accomplish *just for that one day*, and in the evening, of what the day's experience was, and particularly of *what he learned that day*. From there, your agreement may evolve into a more formal statement of your major longer-term goals and strategies.

The content of the agreement, as you'll see, is far less important than the fact that *you have a clear, written understanding of where you're going* **together.**

# Nick

"

But just before we plunge into the real "how-to" of our methods, I want to make sure that you—the advisor's life partner—have some sense of how genuinely thrilling her career can be.

No one tells our partners this stuff, and as often as not even we advisors can't put it into words. But what we do is so personally satisfying, and so terribly important in the lives of our clients, that you can't really appreciate what drives us without understanding it.

We don't just sell insurance and investments. *We sell financial peace.* If our clients die or become disabled, their families won't lose their homes, and their children will still be able to afford a good education. If they live, we'll help them invest so that the kids won't still be paying off student loans when they're fifty years old. We can show people

**We don't sell insurance and investments. We sell financial peace.**

how to invest for a long and worry-free retirement, in such a way that their money outlives them instead of them outliving their money. We can insure them against the risk of long nursing home stays that wipe out all their savings, as well as their legacies to their children.

Above all, we can help them make, and stick to, a long-term financial plan. And that's just something virtually no household/family can do for itself. People know that they can buy insurance and investments online. But they also intuitively know that they can't make a comprehensive financial plan online; they have to sit looking into a financial planner's eyes to do that.

And we can do all that in the context of a purely entrepreneurial business that we can build to suit our own talents and personalities. We may have managers, but in no sense will we ever have a boss who can tell us what to do, and when and where to do it. The degree of freedom this career gives us is intoxicating—as is the potentially limitless income. *All of that—and the only thing we have to give up in return is a salary.*

Think about the courage—and the tremendous desire to succeed on her own terms—your life partner must have in order to make that deal.

And all she has to do all day for years is basically to jump out of the bushes at total strangers, offer to take over the management of their financial lives, and listen to almost everyone say no.

That isn't something anyone should be asked to do alone.

# Joan

Those are all fair comments, and they tell you what motivates Nick (and everyone else who persists until he's successful), as well as why they love their calling so much. This just makes common sense: after all, no one could possibly succeed in a business that generates so much adversity unless he loved it, and believed passionately that he could be a force for good in the world.

But I would quickly caution you not to start thinking that you have to become a student of the business—in other words, don't fall victim to the illusion that you have to understand what your partner does in order to help him do it. *Far from it.*

Full disclosure: most months, I don't even read Nick's newsletter. When I do, I'm always knocked out by it, and I think the subscribers are getting huge value. But I don't need to study it to appreciate it, any more than, in 1969, I needed to understand the economy or the markets to help him deal with the rejection and the adversity he had to face on a daily basis. I had love, and our shared goals—as I'm sure you do. That was enough, and more than enough, to build on. ***All we needed to do was to develop a method of working together productively.***

This we did, and we're about to tell you how.

# 4

# Just for Today

# Nick

"

To recap: the glory of the business is your partner's unlimited potential to do well by doing good for her clients. The price of that glory is her willingness to hear "no" almost all the time, possibly for several years, as she builds her business.

I'm hoping that you've already realized that the key word in that second sentence—and the very essence of the nature of prospecting— is *"**almost**." Almost* everyone your partner approaches cold may decline her healing counsel, *but not quite everyone will.* It's a numbers game. And all successful advisory practices are built on a growing accumulation of the few people who didn't say no—who listened, who found thereby some measure of financial peace, and who introduced your partner to others who needed her counsel.

No one can fail in this business—and in fact there is no limit to what one can achieve— unless and until they stop prospecting.

What Joan and I discovered was that it became infinitely easier for me to keep prospecting—to maintain faith that the law of the golden "almost" was *inevitably* grinding out a successful practice for me— if we would meet every day, in a spirit of perfect harmony, to make a plan for the day in the morning, and to review the day's experiences and lessons at night.

# Joan

"

The intelligence that we've talked about—
the one that is far greater than either or both
of our individual intelligences—is also the
source of far more faith, courage and persistence than either of us had. *But we found that
we could only access it together.*

We need you to know right this minute,
before you read another page, that this
intelligence is no less *potentially* available to
the two of you than it was (and is) to us.

I can't stress this enough: ***don't idealize us.***
Don't think we had anything you two don't,
because it isn't true. We had each other, and
virtually nothing else. That turned out to be
all we needed, and *that's* my whole point.
If we two could build what we have from
nothing, and in some ways less than nothing,
so can you. If you start thinking that we had
some inner qualities or some magic formula
that's unavailable to you, you're already
formulating a rationale for failure, although
you may not be conscious of this.

We met once in the morning, and once in
the evening, for thirty minutes each.

We accept the possibility that you and your
partner may be of a temperament, and
may have enough discipline—or may just
be under so much time pressure—that you
can generate the desired effect with one such
meeting a day, either morning or evening.
In fact, we're perfectly flexible not just with
respect to this issue, but to the length of time
*and even to the content* of your meeting.

Where we are inflexible, and even rigid, is in the belief that the meeting(s) *must take place every single business day at the same time(s)*. This is the key to everything we've ever done successfully, including—as you may already have guessed—writing this book together.

> **66**
>
> **Where we are inflexible, and even rigid, is in the belief that the meeting(s) must take place every single business day at the same time(s).**

Yes, life happens. One morning, one of you—or one of the kids—will wake up with a tummy virus. And one evening, your boss may need you to work late on a project. Sometimes, and maybe more, your morning and/or evening meeting will legitimately have to be scrubbed. But if the meetings are still regularly scheduled, and you both remain wholeheartedly committed to them, you'll be all right.

What they can never be is sporadic, occasional, or hit-and-miss. Those are symptoms of one or both of you not really wanting it, and weak desire will always produce weak results...until, inevitably, the meetings cease altogether. (At which point, should it happen, what do you do? Of, course: meet to determine why it didn't work. Agree on whatever adjustments are necessary to make it work. Re-commit to the new formula. And start over again. In the end, persistence may be all you have. But that's fine, because it's all you need.)

# Nick

The other thing your business meeting can never be is a forum for any and every other conflict in your personal lives and your relationship. Deal with those issues in your own way and on your own time. They are outside the scope of this book, and in fact they're way beyond Joan's and my competence.

The high-functioning business partnership we envision for you, as well as access to the intelligence that makes itself available only to such partnerships, is not premised on some dreamy ideal of the perfect relationship—

**The other thing your business meeting can never be is a forum for any and every other conflict in your personal lives and your relationship.**

which we certainly did not and do not have, and which we don't believe exists.

But if you come to the morning meeting still seething about something her dreadful mother said at dinner last night, or she comes to it resentful that you're still not hauling your fair share of the parenting or the maintenance of the home, it's all over. Don't bother having the meeting. In fact there's no point in even trying to have it, because the higher intelligence you claim to be seeking will already have picked up on your bad vibes, and checked out. Meet in harmony and unconflicted common purpose, or don't meet at all.

# Joan

This brings us to the question of the content of the meeting. The most liberating thing I can tell you is that content just doesn't matter all that much.

That is, there's no objectively right or wrong format or agenda for your meeting. Almost all of the power that's unleashed in both of you by this exercise is generated simply by the cosmic habitforce of the meeting itself. The two of you, together with that higher intelligence, will ultimately work out the ideal agenda.

We can make some suggestions as to things you may want to try, and are about to do so. But take care to stay out of the way of the miracle: the meeting is occasionally (and when you least expect it) going to produce flashes of inspiration that neither of you brought into it.

Sometimes you'll generate an idea about what your partner should say to a particular prospect he's going to see that day. Another time you'll ask him a really interesting question that he'll want to turn around and ask all his prospects. You need to give those epiphanies room to happen, and you can't do that if the meeting is too tightly organized. Trust yourselves.

I'm not making this up. One Thanksgiving in those early years, it was just Nick, me and baby Karen in our little apartment in Brooklyn Heights. We put her to bed after dinner, and—if only for the discipline—sat down for our evening meeting. Nick was dreading going to the office the next day: even though the markets were open on the Friday after the holiday, he'd convinced himself that everybody worth prospecting was probably making a weekend of it, and he wouldn't be able to reach anyone.

The talk somehow turned to his biggest prospect at the time, who lived and had founded

**"**

*Sometimes you'll generate an idea about what your partner should say to a particular prospect he's going to see that day.*

a public company in suburban Philadelphia. Nick had been calling this gentleman, and he was convinced that his firm could be of real service to the man's company, but they had never met. I opened my mouth and heard myself say, "Don't go to the office tomorrow. Get in the car first thing in the morning, get a gas station map, and just…go there. Meet him if you can, and learn more about him and his company even if you can't. But take a positive action." He did, and came back with an account that was very significant to us for the next several years.

Where did that come from?

I certainly didn't bring that idea into the meeting. I never even had the idea until it just popped out that way. But as soon as it did, I knew it was right, and so did Nick. And I'm convinced to this day that it would never have happened if we hadn't had the Meeting Habit. It forces you to expect good things, and that's half the battle.

# Nick

If you have not already figured this out, or if I haven't made it sufficiently clear yet, then let me spell out for you exactly what Joan's Thanksgiving parable confirms. Simply stated, it is that, back then, she had more faith in me than I had in myself. If and to the extent that I ultimately succeeded—beyond my wildest dreams ***but not beyond hers***—it is because she made a decision to believe in the inevitability of that success until I could learn to believe in it myself.

**If and to the extent that I ultimately succeeded, it is because she made a decision to believe in the inevitability of that success.**

I said earlier that, when we committed to working together every day—and thereby to summon that third mind we keep talking about—the possibility of failure ceased to exist. That happened pretty much in a flash for Joan, but it didn't for me. It was a chain that I had to forge every day—one link in the morning and another in the evening—through constant repetition. I don't think it's an oversimplification, much less an overstatement, to sum up those first seven bitter years in one sentence: ***Her faith ultimately drove out my fear.***

You—our reader, the advisor's life partner—may wish to pause for a moment, and consider this. We are not here to impose that same burden on you. Rather, we want simply to put you in touch with the tremendous power you have to influence (and perhaps even to determine) the ultimate outcome of your partner's career.

# Joan

You can't *want* it more than he does; that wouldn't be fair to you, and more importantly, it will never work. But you can believe in it more than he does...*until he does.*

# 5

# Setting
# the
# Agenda

# Nick

**"**

Reading over what we've written so far, I'm concerned that we may seem to be addressing very narrowly the partners of advisors who are new to the industry, and who are just in the early building stages. Nothing could be further from the truth. Speaking for myself, I'm just as eager—and maybe even more so— to reach the partner of the mid-career advisor who is becalmed.

Even among the thinned-out ranks of advisors

who get through the first stage of a career—
the D-Day soldiers who make it off the beach;
the ones who survive those first five years in
production—there are far too many with stunt-
ed, blighted careers. That is, they may have
survived, but they're nowhere near thriving. I
regard this as a tragedy. And I know exactly
how it happens.

They stop prospecting.

But why would an advisor ever do that,
before she had achieved all her dreams?
The answer is that she got to a plateau—
some kind of a comfort zone where she was
making enough money so that survival was
no longer the issue, but real prosperity and
affluence were still a long way off. And once
there, she started to get too comfortable—
and to remember how arduous prospecting
had been.

Little by little, her effort to continue growing her business by offering to bring financial
peace to more people slacked off. Gradually,

she lost her access to the energy that's re-
leased by the realization that the more good an
advisor does—and the more people she does
it for—the wealthier she becomes, and the
more she can do for those she loves.

The problem is that there's really no such thing
as a plateau in this business. It's just the mo-
mentary top before a long downward spiral.

> **There's really no such thing as a plateau in this business. It's just the momentary top before a long downward spiral.**

The less prospecting the advisor does, the
less she finds she can do. In the emotional
void that results, fear creeps back in: she
starts to think, albeit unconsciously, that she
may no longer have what it takes to prospect
in volume. So she tells herself that she's "too

busy." (Too busy to prospect? That's like saying you're too busy to breathe.)

When she tries sporadically to throw herself back into prospecting, the shock of "no"
seems to contain much higher voltage—it
hurts much more—than it did on the first go-
around. This just accelerates the downward

## Too busy to prospect? That's like saying you're too busy to breathe.

spiral, which ends, every single time, in zero
prospecting. And that, sooner or later, trans-
lates into zero career growth, *or worse.*

How does the advisor's partner not know this
(or claim not to know it)? The short answer is
that she's too ashamed to tell you, and—since
you don't have your daily meetings anymore, *if
you ever did*—you don't have a forum in which

to ask. And there never seems to be a right time to bring it up.

But you know. The day you mention that dream you two had years ago, to go on safari in the Serengeti before all the animals are gone, and she says you could get the same effect by going to Florida's Lion Country Safari, you know. The day you say that this *must* be the time to finally buy that cabin on the lake—because home prices and mortgage rates will never be lower again in your lifetimes—and she says maybe next year, you know. The day she comes home with an annual W-2 earnings statement that's an exact replica of the one she brought home *three or more years ago*...**you know**.

Call a meeting. At the meeting, read **together** the section of my prospecting book **The Game of Numbers** dealing with comfort zones, plateaus, and how to re-start the prospecting engine in mid-career. (Don't worry: your partner already has the book, and if she doesn't she certainly knows about it, and where to get it. It's like **Think and Grow Rich**, up there at the top of that closet in Brooklyn Heights, forty-odd years ago: Joan may not have known it was there before it fell on her head, *but I sure did.)*

My whole point is simply that this book is every bit as much for the partner of the advisor who needs to ***re-start*** a career as it is for the partner of the newbie.

# Joan

66

And now, if nobody minds, I'd like to get back to the subject at hand, which—as nearly as I can remember—was creating productive agendas for your morning and evening meetings, *regardless of where in his career your partner may be.*

In its very simplest form, the agenda for the morning meeting should be (a) who your partner plans to see, and/or (b) who he plans to call, and/or just (c) what number of **attempts** to start a prospecting conversation he is going to make, together with (d) roughly what he plans to say...**today.**

The drop-dead critical word in that sentence is, of course, **today**.

This quickly became one of Nick's and my core beliefs. In our attempt to leach as much anxiety out of the prospecting process as we possibly could, we decided (or just accepted) that *it was absolutely impossible for him to make a prospecting approach either yesterday or tomorrow*, or any other day but today. Yesterday is gone; no sense thinking about it. And he couldn't make a prospecting call tomorrow until tomorrow got here, by which time it would have become... that's right...*today.*

Yes, the mortgage payment is going to come due at the end of the month, as is the car payment. And yes, pretty soon baby is going to need a new pair of shoes, or whatever. But not **today**, and therefore none of that gets anywhere near the agenda, because it would only prove distracting at best and anxiety-increasing at worst—both of which we're trying to avoid.

There was only one real question for us every morning. And that was: who would he call (or, again, how many people would

> *There was only one real question for us every morning. And that was: who would he call (or, again, how many people would he attempt to call), who would he see (or attempt to see), and what would he say?*

he attempt to call), who would he see (or attempt to see), and what would he say, if he knew that today had the potential to be the most productive—or at least the most instructive—day of his career so far? **Because, as we had to keep reminding**

**each other every morning, it always had the potential to be both.**

In the evening, we met to go over what he had accomplished relative to his stated intentions that morning *in terms of activity rather than in terms of results*. We also tried to write down one important thing that he had learned that day, even (and especially) from a so-called "failed" sales interview. Because, you see, we clung to the belief that *there was no such thing as a "failed" sales interview,* irrespective of whether the prospect bought anything or not.

We came to understand—and I pray that you will find this a blessing—that the only "failed" sales interview, or cold call, or drop-in, or whatever, was the one *he didn't make because he feared that someone would say "no."*

6

# Measuring Activity, Not "Results"

# Nick

I'm the career financial services professional, with 45 years and eleven books behind me. But I can tell you that most of what I've ever learned about prospecting and sales is implicit in the couple of hundred words Joan just wrote to you.

And I know it's a healing for her to be able to share those truths with you, because you can be sure that no one ever told them to her—or me, for that matter. We had to walk the floors of hell, hanging on to each other for dear life, in order to work them out.

Like everybody else who ever came into the personal financial advice business (especially the four out of five who failed, because this is exactly *why* they failed), I was trained to set my goals in terms of production: how much commission did I generate, how many accounts did I open. I'm sure my counterparts on the insurance side were taught to count only premiums written.

But those turned out to be variables over which, on a day-to-day basis, I had next to no control.

Not only that, but the method of keeping score only by outcomes implicitly forced me to conclude that only "yes" was a success and that therefore "no" must represent a failure. Then I was sent out to begin high-volume prospecting, a task in which I was guaranteed to hear "no"—as we have vividly and repeatedly already seen—almost all the time.

Given that soul-murdering paradigm, the wonder isn't that four out of five new advisors get crushed by it within five years. The wonder is that the casualty rate isn't even higher.

# Joan

Let's say he went out in the morning, determined to call twenty prospects with an investment idea that he loved. And he did call them. Five weren't going to be in their offices at all today; he left his number for five more, but no one called him back; eight said a flat "no;" and two said they'd "think about it" and let him know. If we're keeping score by outcomes, he's going to feel like he ran the gauntlet all day, and got whacked with twenty tomahawks.

So as he now walks back into the house, if my first question is, "How much commission did you make today?" I'm no part of his solution; I'm just another very big part of his problem.

I'm the twenty-first tomahawk.

# Nick

In this example, given the way Joan and I ultimately learned to keep score, I had a spectacularly successful day. Most important, I kept my morning commitment—which wasn't how many orders I was going to get, but *how many genuine attempts I was going to make to tell my story that day.* (Note that by that standard I was a perfect twenty for twenty.)

We knew that prospecting is a numbers game. (That is, we believed in that golden "almost.") And we knew that as I gradually built up the number of genuine prospecting approaches I could make each day—which just meant the number of times I could stand to hear "no" ***and still keep going***—I was getting closer and closer to "yes"—and to a glorious career.

So our meeting that night was a celebration of my (very) slowly increasing endurance. And, as we've said, we made sure to write down one thing I thought I'd learned that day—even if it was an objection I heard again and again. Because tomorrow I would take that objection to the biggest producer in my office, find out how

> **We made sure to write down one thing I thought I'd learned that day—even if it was an objection I heard again and again.**

he would have handled it, and write that down, so it would never stump me again.

## Joan

Of course, one of the reasons he'd gone out that first morning so confident in his sales presentation was that—as part of our morning meeting—he'd rehearsed it. He had written it out the night before (because that's another way he managed his considerable anxiety about talking to wealthy people), and he made the presentation to me just the way he was going to try to make it twenty times that day.

> **Just by adding the rehearsal to our morning meeting, he went out more confident—which we knew was going to give him the strength to absorb even more "no."**

Sometimes I could serve as a useful proxy for the prospect, by spotting something in the presentation that I didn't understand, or that I thought might turn people off. But even when I couldn't—when the presentation made perfect sense to me—he had gotten to hear himself say it out loud, and that got him excited about it all over again.

Just by adding the rehearsal to our morning meeting, he went out more confident—which we knew was going to give him the strength to absorb even more "no."

# Nick

There are two separate themes in what you've just read, and we want to make sure you focused on both of them.

One is the critical importance of our daily meetings, and how they began to evolve—adding such refinements as a presentation rehearsal, and always looking for what we could learn from the day's experiences that might make me stronger and smarter tomorrow.

The other is the whole idea of keeping score in terms of positive actions—a slowly expanding capacity to perform more and more of *the behaviors that lead to success*—rather than by outcomes.

Did I pick up the phone to call a prospect, and was he out at a funeral, and did he not call me back? (Or was he there, and he said "no"?) *I'm a winner.* I had no control over where he was, or what he said. All I could control is all I could

**All I could control is all I could control: placing or not placing the call. I placed it.**

control: placing or not placing the call. I placed it. (I might not have wanted to, but I had committed to Joan just that morning that I would, hadn't I?)

By my scorekeeping method, I took another step today toward my inevitable success. Meanwhile, the advisor in the cubicle next to mine—a guy I think of as being much smarter than I am—had exactly the same experience. But he believed the lie: he keeps score only by outcomes. *In his mind* (and only there), he just got whacked with a tomahawk.

We had the very same experience. He elected to process the experience as a failure. I elected to process it as a success. *We both had that choice.* And one day I'm going to look over there, to discover that that cubicle is empty.

It's never about what happens to your partner. It's about how you and your partner ***together*** choose to process the experience.

7

# The Supreme Secret of Prospecting: "No" Doesn't Hurt

# Joan

"

The epiphany for us came when we discovered that we had perfect control over whether or not to allow "no" to hurt. When we found that out, not only did we decide not to let it hurt; we chose to experience every "no" as a kind of victory, or at the very least a measurable step toward success.

We had already gotten that Nick could not possibly fail unless he stopped prospecting, that if he persisted he must ultimately succeed.

We had also gotten the golden "almost"—
that prospecting was a numbers game, in
which, although *almost* everyone might seem
to be saying "no," *not quite everyone was.*

I'd have been a lot happier, and I know he
would have too, if someone would have just
told us even roughly how many "no" Nick

> *I had had to swear off self-pity—it
> was the only way I could survive.*

needed to hear in order to get to one "yes."
But nobody could, so we just went on. If we
couldn't manage the incidence of "no" per
"yes," then about the only choice we had
was how to process the experience of "no."

He could, and sometimes did, come home
and say something like, "I ran the gauntlet
all day and fifty people buried their toma-

hawks in my head." I admit that this had at some point begun to grate on me. (I had had to swear off self-pity—*it was the only way I could survive*—and was therefore perhaps not perfectly tolerant of it in him.) So without wishing to seem at all unsympathetic, one evening I mentioned to Nick that I had looked carefully, and there were no tomahawks in his head. Nor was I able to detect any obvious tomahawk wounds.

Wouldn't you know it? This became the subject for that night's meeting.

# Nick

"

This reads funnier than it actually was, but
the point was well taken. Once we sat down
and talked it over, we decided that it was very
improbable that any of the fifty people I had
called that day had any memory of the inter-
action. None of them could pick me out of a
police lineup, and I was pretty sure that none
of them could even remember my name. I
offered my services, such as they were; that
day, each person said "no." (If I was honest, I
had to admit that some were perfectly pleas-

ant about it: said they had good investment advice, thanked me and then hung up before I could tell them that nobody has a monopoly on good investment ideas—or whatever I'd been trained to say.)

These people had not, in any objective way, inflicted any pain on me. *But I genuinely felt pain.* There seemed only one plausible explanation:

> **Once we sat down and talked it over, we decided that it was very improbable that any of the fifty people I had called that day had any memory of the interaction.**

*in my fear, insecurity and—yes—self-pity, I had manufactured the pain. I had elected to experience something—"the pain of rejection"—that had no reality **other than that which I chose to give it.***

The next day I went into the office, turned my chair around, and watched the most successful producer in the office call people. He did it all morning. Made a heck of a lot more calls than I did; seemed to be hearing "no" way more than I did. But the smile never left his face. He just didn't let it bother him. When I plucked up the courage to ask him about this, he simply said, "It's a numbers game; this is what we have to do to be successful. There's no other way, so I don't see the sense of getting emotional about it."

I got that.

# Joan

The next step was to realize that if we had a choice not to let "no" be a painful experience—if indeed it had no emotional weight at all other than what Nick chose to give it—then we could elect to see every "no" as a positive, another step toward an inevitable "yes," after which the process would repeat itself.

Sometime after *that*, we learned (from the sales psychologist Aaron Hemsley, whose CDs—they were tapes then—I still live by) that we could count as a success even the *attempt* to risk a "no." Aaron claimed that if Nick so much as dialed the phone and got a busy signal, he had had a winning experi-

> *We learned (from the sales psychologist Aaron Hemsley, whose CDs—they were tapes then—I still live by) that we could count as a success even the attempt to risk a "no."*

ence: he had genuinely tried to risk hearing a "no," in the sure and certain knowledge that that was the only way in the world he would ever get to hear a "yes."

That made instant, total and perfect sense to me.

# Nick

And in time, it made sense to me, too, if only because I couldn't evade the logic of it, which seemed to go like this:

(a) I can do limitless good for people, and earn limitless rewards for myself and my family, by offering people the financial peace they crave and cannot achieve on their own.

(b) The only way I can possibly avoid these glorious outcomes is if I stop prospecting.

(c) But I would only stop prospecting if I were to be defeated by "the pain of rejection."

(d) And "the pain of rejection" doesn't exist, other than in my mind. I not only permit it, I create it. But now I see that it is a delusion, and I relinquish it.

(e) In its place, I elect to create something else, or more accurately to tune my consciousness to another frequency: that is, to the higher, finer, purer intelligence that never fails to manifest itself when Joan and I meet in perfect harmony to summon it.

Four decades later, I saw a television commercial featuring Michael Jordan, one of the most accomplished athletes who ever lived. He says:

> **"I've missed nine thousand shots in my career.**
>
> **"I've lost almost three hundred games.**
>
> **"Twenty-six times, I've been trusted with the ball to take the game-winning shot.**
>
> **"And missed.**
>
> **"I've failed over and over and over again in my life.**
>
> **"And that is why I succeed."**

8

# Your Partner Is Going To Succeed

# Joan

Make no mistake about it: your partner has a gift. He and you have set yourselves to the noble work of doing well by doing good, which is the whole financial planning profession summed up in five words. By this point, you and he are committed to his daily practice of building up over time his capacity to prospect, knowing that success can't possibly be denied to the advisor who never stops prospecting. The outcome of these last three sentences (which I invite you to read again) can be only one thing: *your partner is going to be successful.*

At this point, it seems to me that we've accurately described the genuinely hard work of being the partner of someone who's building (or rebuilding) a financial advisory practice. It was extremely important to me, especially,

> ## *The struggle is not the goal, and success is much more than the failure to fail.*

to do that for you: to prepare you in no uncertain terms for the experiences you must anticipate, *as no one prepared me.*

But the struggle is not the goal, and success is much more than the failure to fail.

This is not a footnote, or even an aside. In

fact, it's the sum of the book so far, so please don't rush past it. If this little book has succeeded to this point, we've brought you to a state where you now realize that failure is impossible. I'd just like you to rest in the shade of that truth for a moment. And realize that the remainder of your journey is going to be that much easier—regardless of how long it takes—because you and your partner share the confidence that you're going to get to your destination.

The question now becomes: where is that destination?

# Nick

**"**

In other words, what are your goals—*your shared, mutually agreed upon, clearly written down and reviewed every day goals?*

Most people seem to do the goal-setting process backwards, which goes a long way to an understanding of why most people flunk out of the business altogether, or barely manage to survive in a grey twilight that is neither outright failure nor genuine success.

That is, they set all kinds of big, dreamy, ideal long-term goals without giving any real thought to the day-to-day mindset and behaviors necessary to the achievement of those goals. This is no more valid than a new year's resolution: I'm going to lose thirty pounds by my birthday in October—with no specific enumeration of the daily changes in diet and exercise requisite to that goal.

One pound of fat equals 3,500 calories; did you know that? So if you want to lose thirty pounds in nine months, you'll have to forgo close to four hundred calories a day (or burn that many calories in increased exercise) *every day from January 1 to October 1* in order to achieve your goal. (And prospecting is an order of magnitude tougher, because, unlike calories per pound, *you can't even know how many "no" you'll need to hear in order to get to one "yes."*)

Understand me: I certainly don't have anything *against* goal-setting. Indeed, how else would you know where you're trying to go? (And as the great Zen master Yogi Berra said, "If you don't know where you're going, you might not get there.") I'm just dead set against *goal-setting as an end in itself,* with insufficient attention paid to the behavioral disciplines that are necessary to the goal.

# Joan

Fair enough, but I still think you need to be working toward a definite goal all the time. I can remember when our second daughter Joanie was outgrowing her bassinet, and we needed to get her a real crib. Our goal— written down and recited every morning before Nick went out the door—was that baby Joan must have her crib now. We even had the catalog picture of the exact crib we wanted for her, pasted (along with the price) to the top of our statement.

Today, our goals may be far more ambitious than a beautiful, sturdy crib. *But we still have clear, specific goals to which we are committed **together**.* The goal that we're aiming toward in any given year is written down, and we recite it every morning. When Nick is traveling to a speaking engagement, we recite it on the phone. (You will find the formula we use for our statement of purpose, as well as a formula for developing the self-confidence needed to achieve that purpose, in *Think and Grow Rich*. You don't have to re-invent that wheel.)

Again, from the deepest experience: *your partner's time is coming*. To doubt that, even in the darkest hours, is to doom it. I could have gone back to my Wall Street position in a heartbeat when he was struggling. But I believed then, and I believe now, that he might never have made it—certainly not on the scale that he ultimately did—had we surrendered to that doubt and fear. My election to be a stay-at-home mom was not, in that sense, merely a lifestyle choice. *It was an act of faith.*

# 9

## Fear Kills

# Nick

"

There are really only two emotions you and your partner can bring to this endeavor. One is faith, and the other is fear. Our experience is that they're mutually exclusive, and perfectly so. That is, you don't wake up in the morning with a blend of, say, 70% faith and 30% fear in your emotional gas tank, or 70%/30% the other way. Or any other fear/faith mixture. You wake up in the morning fueled by one emotion or the other. If it's the wrong one, you can sit down to your morning meeting with your partner, drain the tank, refuel with the right stuff, and start your day.

If you believe what we've told you so far, you have faith in the inevitability of your partner's success. Fear is therefore absent, because it isn't credible. To fear is to accept the possibility that an obvious lie—"she can prospect all day every day until the crack of doom and she can still fail"—is true. This is irrational in the extreme. It may be all too human, and it completely explains failure, but it's irrational.

Fear is a self-fulfilling prophecy. It drives out faith. Then it takes away your voice. Then it isolates and immobilizes you. And then it kills you. And that's not even the bad news.

The bad news is that you had a choice. Fear did not sneak up on you. It didn't take you down from behind. It isn't encoded in your genetic material. It isn't hereditary, or even environmental. It's a choice you make.

Emmet Fox tells the story of a hunting party

out west that had pitched camp as the sun was setting, and started supper. Just then, they became aware of the presence of game nearby, and hastily went in search of it, leaving a kettle of water coming to a boil over the fire.

"Presently an old bear crept out of the woods, and, seeing the kettle with its lid

**Fear is a self-fulfilling prophecy. It drives out faith. Then it takes away your voice. Then it isolates and immobilizes you. And then it kills you. And that's not even the bad news.**

dancing about on top, promptly seized it. The boiling water scalded him badly; but instead of dropping the kettle instantly, he proceeded to hug it tightly—this being the bear's idea of defense. Of course, the tighter he hugged it the more it burned him; and the more it burned the tighter he hugged it; and so on in a vicious circle, to the undoing of the bear."

In this fable, the boiling water is fear, and you guys are the bear. Except that, although fear may be as instinctive in you as the bear hug was to the bear, you still have a choice. The bear hasn't got a mind to change. You and your partner do. I was, as I've said, blessed to have a partner whose faith ultimately drove out my fear—who kept knocking that kettle out of my grasp until I didn't need her to anymore. You can't do that forever. And you can't do it if your partner, because of her own pathology, won't let you. But you can do it. Please reflect on this.

# Joan

But you can't do it if you yourself have surrendered to fear. I never really did. I can't
explain why, even now—there was certainly
nothing in my background that would have
predicted my faith in Nick, in the business
and in the future. The faith must always
have been there, but it didn't crystallize into
a force until that book fell on my head.

When it did, a switch flipped. I must always have
thought that poverty was a human invention,

a story that people tell themselves about themselves, and that they persist in believing even though it's so clearly not true. I somehow knew that poverty and failure were lies, and I came to discover that, deep down, I had never believed the lies. I pray that you don't either. But if you do, you can stop. Indeed, you *must* stop.

# Nick

I find that a lot of people who are struggling in the business spend a lot of time and energy trying to figure out what it is that they're afraid *of*, as if that were going to get them any closer to conquering the fear. Permit me to suggest that this is ultimately navel-gazing.

Is fear of poverty materially different, in its causes and effects, from the fear of ill health, or of criticism, or even of death? Are these pathologies separable from each other in any practical, useful way—a way that might enable you to isolate and kill one using a different strategy than you would against another? I don't think so.

And for that matter—on an even higher plane—is the fear of failure identifiably and importantly different from the fear of success? My friend Steven Pressfield certainly thinks it is. In his classic and indispensable book *The War of Art*—which liberated me to write my own prospecting book, *The Game of Numbers*—he tracks all fears back to the fear of success: to the mortal terror that we achievers feel about risking everything in order to become all that we were created capable of being. And for all I know, he may even be right.

My position is: I'll never know for sure, so I have elected not to care. (Thank heaven, I've just never been into "why.") I simply believe that fear is fear, that it is supremely irrational in the context of what advisors do, and that it will kill us if we don't kill it.

But I know that it can be killed—if only one day at a time—by your and your partner's daily manifestation of the belief that success cannot be denied to anyone who refuses to stop prospecting. (Fear is, of course, acutely aware that this is its Achilles heel—the only way it can be destroyed—which is why it directly, relentlessly and mercilessly attacks your partner's commitment to disciplined prospecting.)

# Joan

I'm not sure I buy all of that. (I don't have to be: *he* bought it, and it set him free. And that was the object of the whole exercise, wasn't it?) But what I absolutely believe is Dr. Hill's assurance that the two roads (of fear leading to failure, and faith leading to success) travel in opposite directions. There can be no compromise. That's what Nick was talking about a few moments ago, with the analogy that your partner's engine won't run on any mixture of fear and faith. You're traveling one road or the other. It's a decision you make every day—and sometimes you'll have to make it every hour.

Note that I didn't just say that *your partner* has to make this decision every day, and maybe every hour. You can't hold him to a higher standard than you hold yourself. The morning meeting isn't just a pep talk, after which he goes out to do battle, and you go back to bed, or whatever. If you genuinely expect him to fight off indecision, doubt and fear, you had better be prepared to do likewise.

I always know that I'm personally going off the beam when I start procrastinating: when I have so many things to do that I'm suddenly aware of how wonderfully effective I'd be if I just started to do them...tomorrow.

I immediately sit down and write myself an email—not just a "to do" list but a schedule of what activity I'm going to tackle at what time today. That's "activity," not necessarily "task": my schedule can and quite often will include taking a well-deserved nap, or getting a pedicure. I'm not trying to get absolutely everything done today. I'm pulling myself back from the brink of anxiety by fixing a reasonable schedule for doing what I can *just today,* task by task—and reward by reward.

# Nick

Something should probably be said here, too, about the constant negativity and fear that are beamed at all of us—literally all day every day—by the 24-hour "news" cycle. Pessimism is the fuel that all journalism runs on; bad news is good copy. If a hundred thousand Girl Scouts across the country bring a Mother's Day rose to a million nursing home-bound elderly mothers, and on the same day there's a house fire somewhere in which two members of a family lose their lives, it will always be the fire that leads the "news."

On an even larger scale—and this is very pertinent to the career of a financial advisor—the financial media are massively focused on everything that's wrong, or that they hope will soon go wrong, in the economy and the markets: inflation, deflation, higher gas prices, falling home prices, volatile stock prices, unemployment, tornados, earthquakes, tsunamis, or just the latest Ponzi schemer apprehended trying to flee the country.

You and your partner must learn—and you will, I promise you—not merely to tune out journalism's Negativity Narrative so that it doesn't infect you, but to see that it greatly adds to the value of your partner's advice. Today's "crisis" always fades away, while the world continues to grow and prosper as never before. Thus, *your partner may be the only voice of rational long-term optimism that a client hears all day.*

For no matter what seems to be going awry in the world, we know that people who patiently save and plan and insure and invest ultimately control their own destinies, and therefore ultimately attain some measure of financial peace—the peace your partner sells.

But you can't sell what you don't have. This is just another reason—if you still needed another—why there's no room for fear of the future in your partnership. People don't need your partner's fear, and they certainly won't pay her for it. They need her faith and courage. Believe in yourselves—believe in each other—and good people will come to believe in both of you.

# 10

# The Illusion of "Motivation"

# Joan

"

When Nick was in training to be a stockbroker—which in those days really just meant a securities salesman—I started to hear a lot about this notion of "motivation." That sales was a tough racket, that one had to be prepared to face a lot of "rejection," and that the thing that got one through was this mysterious substance (or something) called "motivation," which some people somehow had enough of, and others didn't, with no apparent rhyme or reason.

This made zero sense to me. I thought, frankly, that the guy was motivated enough for about three lifetimes.

He obviously loved me, and the children as they came along. He had had an excellent (if still incomplete) education, knew about the finer things of life, and really wanted those things for us and for himself. He was intensely aware that selling investment advice was a way to build one's own fortune by helping other people build theirs, a concept he found tremendously exciting. He knew himself to be bright, well spoken and persuasive. Finally, he was simply haunted by the failure of his father, whom he considered a tragically wasted talent, to provide well for his family, and Nick was passionately determined—I may say *driven*—to provide well for his own.

Whatever problems he was experiencing in those early years, I couldn't see that a lack of "motivation" was one of them, much less the critical one.

# Nick

"

Years later, when we discovered Aaron Hemsley's "Psychology of Maximum Sales Production" tapes, we were relieved to hear Aaron totally laugh off the whole idea of "motivation." He said, in effect, that anyone who would spurn the security of a salary in order to dictate his own income—which he would then earn entirely through his own intelligence and effort—is not merely sufficiently motivated: ***he (or she) is a super-achiever.***

That was the good news. The bad news, Aaron suggested, was that super-achievers get that way to compensate for a perceived lack of approval and appreciation in their early lives. (I could relate.) He said we're still unconsciously searching for that missing approval—so that when somebody buys our life

**Super-achievers get that way to compensate for a perceived lack of approval and appreciation in their early lives.**

insurance policy or our recommended mutual fund, we find a little bit of it.

The trouble with *that,* in turn, is that if we have vested in other people the power to approve of us, we've also given them the power to tell us—by the act of saying "no"—that we are lacking, inadequate, and wanting. And since "no" is almost all we're going to hear for a long time, it is exactly the approval-starved personality of the super-achiever which is most susceptible to being crushed by "the pain of rejection."

As we've seen, that wholly imagined hyper-sensitivity is the thing we have to work on, not our "motivation."

# Joan

"Not enough motivation" is worse than an alibi: it's a misdiagnosis. Get over it. Tell your partner, in no uncertain terms, to get over it. That dog simply will not hunt.

# 11

# The Strange Case of Family and "Friends"

# Joan

**"**

As you and your partner embark on the glorious entrepreneurial adventure of doing well by doing good, you may have occasion to be somewhat surprised at the reaction of family and "well-meaning friends." These surprises may not always be positive, because the people around you may not be quite as enthusiastic and supportive as you might have expected them to be.

You probably won't have seen this coming,

and your innocence in this regard says really good things about you. But your and your partner's courage and commitment—to his practice, *and especially to each other*—can't help but make people look at themselves. And they may be less than totally enchanted by what they see.

When Nick and I were struggling in our mid-to-late 20s, many or most of my girl-friends from high school and college were marrying young men who were following the most prized career path of that era: getting secure jobs with big companies—jobs which they hoped and expected to have through-out their working lives. My maid of honor, in particular, had married a lovely guy who went straight out of college into a job sell-ing advertising (on salary) for the largest and most prestigious media company of that time. Their first daughter was born about a year before our Karen.

One day I invited her and her daughter to our little apartment in Brooklyn Heights.

It was apparent—and I certainly made no attempt to hide—that we were in financially straitened circumstances. But I was proud of my faith in Nick, and I wanted my friend to be proud of me, too.

> ❝
>
> *I was proud of my faith in Nick, and I wanted my friend to be proud of me, too.*

Instead, all she could talk about was how grim everything seemed to be for us. And when I put out our modest lunch, she asked me—these were her exact words—if I weren't sad because I couldn't give my daughter a lamb chop for lunch.

I didn't see my maid of honor for many, many years after that. And that really hurt.

Ditto family, only much more so. (Remember the story of that Thanksgiving when it was only me, Nick and baby Karen? Now you know why.)

I tell you this for the same reason I tell you everything else in my part of this book: so that you will not get blindsided by the realities of the life you and your partner have chosen. Somewhere in his book, Napoleon Hill virtually cries out, *"You cannot afford the luxury of a single negative thought!"* That means you're going to have to shut out every negative influence in your lives if your partner is going to make it. More to the point, you may have to shut out—or very sharply limit your contact with—people who prove to be carriers of that negativity, as it relates to your and your partner's situation.

And don't permit family or "friends" to try to give you guilt about this. The guilt, if any, should be all on their side.

# Nick

**"**

And, after all, consider what people must be seeing when they look at the two of you.

They have jobs which they may or may not like. In those jobs, they have bosses whom they may or may not respect, but who can tell them what to do, whether they like it or not. Those bosses also tell them exactly how much they can earn. Moreover, their jobs can disappear tomorrow: if the great recession of recent years taught us anything, it's that the

only truly secure job is one you make
for yourself.

Your partner has a career, calling on limitless
numbers of prospects who have financial issues which can only be solved by a caring and
competent financial advisor. She can never get
laid off; indeed, the competition to hire advisors with thriving practices only seems to grow
more intense.

You and your partner may be sacrificing now—
but what entrepreneurs *don't* live on coffee
and rice in the early years of building a business? And remember: every luxury forgone,
every dinner out postponed, every vacation not
taken is a direct investment in the business.
And like every good business, that investment
will pay you back in torrents as the years pass.

The business can only grow, providing you
with any income you require of it, so long as
your partner does a commensurate amount
of good. Over and above that current income,
the business will be accreting significant

residual value, which you may decide to realize through the sale of the practice somewhere down the road.

Or you may just go on growing it, to the point where it requires the services and talents of both of you. Indeed, even your children may elect to join you in the business at some point, making it even more productive—and more

**You and your partner may be sacrificing now—but what entrepreneurs don't live on coffee and rice in the early years of building a business?**

attractive to affluent clients who feel more comfortable with the continuity in such a practice. (I know of any number of happy, thriving transgenerational advisory practices. And I can tell you that they are a joy to behold.)

Does any of this sound like *anything* the holder of a salaried job can say?

The people around you are all going to want to—or are going to be forced to—retire someday, and I'll bet you that not one in twenty feels sure he'll have enough to live on for the rest of his life.

**Your partner never has to retire. She may decide to cut back at some point—just to work a couple or three days a week with clients she loves and who love her, in between leisurely vacations.**

Your partner never has to retire. She may decide to cut back at some point—just to work a couple or three days a week with cli-ents she loves and who love her, in between leisurely vacations—but why would anybody ever want totally to retire from doing good? (Not I; that's for sure.)

This is all because you and your partner have risked everything to build something that will grow to be uniquely valuable *and uniquely your own.* Relatively few of the people around you, who never had the smallest part of your courage or ambition, will be able to find it in their hearts to exult for you and cheer you on. This doesn't necessarily make them bad people.

It just makes them human.

# 12

# The Business Is A Virtuous Cycle

# Joan

"

I've long since started feeling as if all I've been doing so far is delivering more or less dire warnings. I can only hope it's obvious that I've done so out of love.

Nick always says that he writes his "how to" books for the industry to one person: the Nick of 1967—the kid who became a stock-broker knowing nothing about stocks, even less about the business of selling them to people, very little about money, and effectively nothing about affluent people themselves. He says he just writes down everything he wishes someone had told that kid, and that no one did.

I guess I've been having pretty much the same experience: I've taken it as my mission in this book to get the advisor's partner ready, with eyes wide open, for the challenges of that life. And if nobody minds, I'd like to be done with that part now. I want to move on to the joys.

The first and most obvious of these is that you get to live with a pretty interesting person, who is in a *very* interesting business. Your partner may be a lot of work (as mine certainly was, *and is*), but he's not usually boring.

Preparatory to writing each of the numbered sections of this book, Nick and I sat across from each other at our partners' desk—the kind Victoria and Albert had, and the kind we always promised ourselves. And he said, "What is the next thing we should talk about in the book, and what do you want the audience to know about it?"

Then just last night he said, "What do you want the advisor's partner to know about *the*

**"**

**He said, "What do you want the advisor's partner to know about the business itself?" And I said, with no hesitation, "Creative. Changeable. Challenging."**

*business itself?"* And I said, with no hesitation, "Creative. Changeable. Challenging."

We've covered a lot—though certainly not all—of the importantly challenging aspects, and I suspect that we'll get to a very few more before we're done. (This is not an encyclopedia; it's a guide.) So I'd like to turn now to the creative and changeable aspects.

If your advisor partner is anything like mine (and like me, for that matter), he has a very low threshold of boredom. This is not somebody who could have worked his way up the corporate ladder for thirty years at, say, PepsiCo, flogging ever larger quantities of sugar water and salty snacks to the multitudes in order to advance his career. He'd have blown his brains out, and I might have helped him.

> *If your advisor partner is anything like mine (and like me, for that matter), he has a very low threshold of boredom.*

He needed a stimulating environment, in which Wednesday was never exactly the same as Tuesday. And heaven knows, in taking on a career of daily trying to make sense of the economy and the markets, that's what he got. The big upside of this is that the

financial world is one of lifelong learning—
that's another way of saying "changeable."
In the business of financial services, there's
always something new.

It's creative because your partner gets to
choose from a whole palette of financial
products and services that go into the cre-
ation of each uniquely personal financial
plan. In that sense, every plan is an original
work of art. My guy needed that, too.

I don't get involved in the technical aspects
of the business; never have. I could never
see the point. This is why I said early in the
book, and now say again, that you don't have
to be any kind of student of the business to
be immensely helpful to your partner. From
my perspective, in fact, just the opposite
was true. That's because I felt that if I tried
to learn all that stuff, in some sense I might
seem to be competing with him—or at least
that's how he might perceive it.

And you and I certainly don't want that.

# Nick

"

This is not to say that Joan was the right brain (emotional, intuitive) partner and I the left brain (analytical, intellectual) one. We were and are both pretty right brain, she even more so than I. She therefore understood sooner than I did that the business is, in its essence, a behavioral virtuous cycle, as follows:

The more attempts I made to start a prospecting conversation, the more prospecting conversations I actually had. The more prospecting conversations I had, the more accounts I opened. The more accounts I opened, the more opportunities I had to do great planning work for people. The more great planning work I did for people, the more money they brought me to manage, and the more people they introduced me to who needed great planning work done for them. The more people who came to me seeking great planning work, the more money I earned, the more fulfilled I felt...and the more my happy clients did my prospecting for me.

That is the virtuous cycle of the financial planning business. And its uncaused cause is the simple attempt to start a conversation—the offer to help. Thus personal financial planning is in its purest essence *a business of doing, not of knowing.*

Counterintuitive, but true. And it tells you why Joan's instinct to be totally uninterested in what she calls "the technical aspects of the business" was more acute than either of us might have realized at the time.

# 13

# Financial Planning Is Fundamentally Simple

# Joan

"

If you are suddenly a financial planner's life partner, and you have never thought about financial planning for ten minutes in your whole life, I guarantee that you could still sit down with a pad and a pencil, and in the space of half an hour—using nothing but your own good common sense— figure out most if not all the major issues in financial planning.

First of all, there can't be that many make-

or-break planning issues. And second, the few there are pretty much jump right out at you.

Case in point: the mother of all financial planning issues. "What happens to the family/household financially if the

> **"**
>
> *There can't be that many make-or-break planning issues. And the few there are pretty much jump right out at you.*

breadwinner dies?" (If there are two bread-winners, as there increasingly are: what happens if either one or the other dies?)

See, that's what I mean: with your good common sense, knowing that the biggest issues have to get defined first, and know-ing you only have half an hour, you would instinctively know that the big issue can't be, just for example, which mutual fund should I buy.

So: the biggest financial planning problem revolves around the issue of untimely death. It always has, and always will, because that's the ultimate wild card. What's next? Again, this should be obvious. If the biggest risk in terms of its potentially disastrous financial effect is the breadwinner waking up dead, the next biggest would have to be: the breadwinner waking up disabled.

Therefore, the first two steps in financial planning must be to insure the risks of death and disability. How much insurance? What kind of insurance? What kinds of disability to insure against? These are details and refinements. We're just solving here for the very few threshold issues.

OK, so now the family/household is reasonably protected financially against the death or disability of the key member or members.

Now assume nobody dies or gets disabled. The adults live out normal lifespans in normal health. What's next?

Well, if there are children, the next thing is probably funding their education. This goal can't be saved for—the return on savings, net of inflation and taxes, is virtually always less than zero—so it has to be invested for. But invested how? Invested in what? Are there tax-favored ways of investing for college? Details and refinements.

The big issues are two: knowing you have to invest instead of saving, *and knowing that your goal—the number of dollars each child will need— is a moving target.* If your daughter is three, and you want her to go to Duke starting fifteen years from now, you can't spend the next fifteen years investing to accumulate today's Duke tuition, because by the time she's ready, it'll probably cost twice what it does now.

Moving target. Common sense. Next?

Well, beyond the kids' college, the next huge issue is our own retirement. What's the nature of the problem? Pretty simple: does the income outlive the people or do the people outlive their income? The former outcome is really good. The latter is really, *really* bad.

Modern two-person retirements are going to be upwards of thirty years long, because the life expectancy of two people together is a lot longer than the life expectancy of either of the two people individually. (OK, so maybe that isn't exactly common sense; maybe it's a fact you have to learn. Once.)

At the inflation rate that's prevailed for upwards of the last ninety years, during a thirty-year retirement the cost of living will go up around two and a half times. If our income doesn't go up two and a half times along with our living costs, we may be looking at Outcome Two, from the paragraph before last.

This is a common sense problem. The so-lution is just a little cleverer than common sense, and it is right up in Nick's wheelhouse, so I'll let him take it up with you in his own good time. My only point is that the problem itself is obvious.

Next is how we're going to defray the cost of nursing home (or full-time in-home) care during the last five years or so of life— when almost half our lifetime medical costs will be incurred. This one is getting huge. Go out to dinner with three 65-year-old couples. I will bet you anything that by the main course, the talk will have turned to the problems some of them are having, caring for their mothers.

We know we don't want to end up being a burden on our kids. We also don't want to wipe out the legacies we've built for them and for the grandchildren, paying for nurs-ing home care. This risk will have to be invested for and/or insured against. Common sense.

Finally, if—please God—we end our lives with some wealth to leave the people we love, how shall we do that in such a way that half or more of it doesn't get taxed away?

I count six issues here, and it's a heck of a lot less than half an hour since we took up this question.

Anybody—including your partner—who tells you that financial planning is fundamentally complex doesn't understand financial planning. In its essence, it's simply responding to any or all of these six bedrock human issues.

Common sense.

# Nick

❝

Financial planning *solutions* can certainly get very complex, and I'll address that issue in a moment. Joan's point is that *the essential issues are very simple, because they're so human.* They ask the two questions: what do we hope will happen, and what do we fear might happen?

The answer to these questions becomes my twenty-word definition of the financial planning process:

*We insure against what can go wrong, in order to acquire the luxury of investing for what can go right.*

To paraphrase Lincoln: whatever approach differs from these twenty words, to the extent of the difference, is no financial plan.

If your partner comes home all excited because she got a new prospect today with $1.4 million in his 401(k) that he needs to roll over, and she has to sit down after dinner and design a portfolio, you have my permission to suspect that the gargoyles have taken over the cathedral. Where is the prospect's will? Where is his written financial and/or estate plan? If the prospect goes under a bus tomorrow morning, what happens to his family?

These are the questions a financial planner worthy of the name would need to know the answers to, before she'd even think about designing a portfolio—which could otherwise just be an exercise in rearranging the deck chairs on the *Titanic*.

This tells you a corollary precept to the basic twenty-word financial planning formula above. To wit, no financial planner ever accepts the management of an investment portfolio *without a written plan.*

Now, what could be simpler or more straightforward than that?

# Joan

These principles may be very important, but before we get too far afield from the essential human simplicities of financial planning, let's not fail to highlight the really big one: *it's morally wrong, and psychologically unsound, for your partner to be out there selling financial planning if he hasn't done a plan for the two of you (and the children, if you have them).*

The morality of his primary obligation to you and the kids should be obvious. I say "psychologically unsound" because if he's preaching what he's failed to practice, he's going to experience a lot of conflict. Conflict drains energy, and energy is exactly what it takes to prospect. By being false to himself and to you in this way, he's setting himself up to fail.

And you know what else? When he tries to sell what he hasn't done for his own, somehow the prospect will feel it, and the bad vibes will make him turn away from your partner—without ever being conscious of what he's reacting to.

Insist on a plan. *Now.*

# 14

# Leaving Expertise to the Experts

# Nick

**❝**

I acknowledged a moment ago that although
the essential human financial planning needs
might be starkly simple, the *solutions* to those
problems could get complex—and in the case
of more affluent clients, perhaps quite complex.

How your partner proposes to discover and
implement those complexities is a huge and
even a defining professional decision for her,
in terms of choosing the best uses for her career time and energy. It may also represent a

major lifestyle decision for the two of you, and for the family.

The essential issue here is the financial advisor's circle of competence. From the moment we enter the business, I believe, we are consciously or unconsciously drawing a circle around ourselves. We stand inside the circle, along with the things we've chosen to try to master, and to be personally responsible for. Outside the circle we place those issues which will have to be addressed in the course of our work, but regarding which we choose to rely on the expertise of others whose job it is to master those complexities.

If we try to bring too many variables inside the circle with us—tax and estate law, economic forecasting, market analysis and securities selection, to name a few—we will defeat ourselves, and be of no use to anyone: it's the jack of all trades, master of none syndrome. Realizing this, we try to establish what we can—or just what we want to—be directly responsible for.

My experience suggests that the quality of your partner's life (professionally, and with you) will be that much higher, the more he leaves expertise to the experts—that is, the more of the technical complexities he consciously places **outside** his own circle of competence.

I'm a salesman of financial planning in my blood and my bones. That means I was sent

> **My experience suggests that the quality of your partner's life (professionally, and with you) will be that much higher, the more he leaves expertise to the experts.**

into the world to help people move toward the solutions to their essential lifetime financial issues. My ego wasn't invested in—and my fortune wasn't built on—how smart I am, or how many technical complexities I'd mastered. I cared most about how empathetic I was, and how many people—responding to that empathy—came to entrust their financial fates to me.

I'm not in the insurance business. I'm not in the investment business. I'm neither an

**I'm in the human nature business. I was sent here to try to inspire people to do with their money what they need to do instead of what they want to do.**

accountant nor a lawyer. In a sense, I'm not even in the financial planning business. ***I'm in the human nature business.*** I was sent here to try to inspire people to do with their money what they need to do instead of what they want to do. It was the noblest calling to which I could have aspired. And it had virtually nothing to do with what I knew.

The "experts," I always found, knew orders of magnitude more than I ever could about the technical complexities, and not a fraction of what I knew about getting people to move, and to do the right thing. Expertise is their core competency, as empathy is mine. The two are almost mutually exclusive, yet they are perfectly complementary. I elected therefore to leave the experts to look into their computer screens, and I spent every possible working moment looking into the eyes of my clients and prospects, which is where all the real work of this profession gets done.

The more you, the financial planner's life partner, can nudge her along toward this epiphany, the more successful she's going to be, and the happier you're going to be.

# Joan

"

There isn't a whole lot I can, or would even
want to, add to that. The essential point is
the one we made, from our own experience,
a few pages back: an advisor always learns by
doing; he can never do by learning. I'm 45
years a salesman's wife, so you'll have to for-
give my biases. But show me an advisor with
six professional designations after his name
on his business card, and I will—as gently
as possible—show you someone who (as my
husband once said) could not sell a glass of

ice water to his own mother in the middle
of Death Valley at high noon on the second
Sunday in August. It's not just a different set
of skills; it's a different way of looking at life.
And never the twain shall meet.

# 15

# Questioning and Listening

# Joan

"

We made the point earlier that Nick and I originally managed his anxiety at presenting investments to affluent people by having him script—word for word, even down to the pauses—everything he was going to say. He would rehearse in our meetings—especially the one on Sunday night, which remains to this day a great tool for us—and I would try to listen to what his prospect was going to hear, to see if it was clear and compelling to me as a proxy for the individual investor.

Over time, as his confidence grew, the need for this technique progressively withered away. I realized that the process was complete one morning when he was going out on a big appointment. I asked, "Do you know what you're going to say?" He said, "Actually, I'm just going to listen to what *they* have to say, and take it from there."

I couldn't have told you exactly why or how, but I knew in that moment he had become the consummate professional he had so desperately wanted to be.

# Nick

"

After those first few awful years, I put aside the broken stockbroker paradigm in which I'd been trained, and began groping my way toward financial planning. But I've always thought of myself more as a professional salesman of financial planning rather than, in any technical sense, a financial planner.

My self-conception was as a communicator, a translator between the clients and the "experts" (who by and large speak different languages), and a highly principled persuader. I sought to show people, in the simplest possible terms, the key decisions they needed to make in order to find financial peace: the gratification they'd have to defer, the thrift they'd have to practice. Then I encouraged them, as best I could, to embrace those decisions.

As my work matured, I no longer had any real doubt that the plan I was offering was right for my prospect. (The "experts" had seen to that.) And in fact I rarely encountered a prospect who said my plan was importantly wrong for his situation. The only question was: would the prospect commit to the plan. That—and not on the plan itself—was where I focused all my energies, because I had discovered almost right away that *people don't really buy the plan; they buy the planner.*

The reason I was so highly confident that the plan was right was twofold. First, I had asked all the right questions: not about dollars and cents, but about hopes and fears. Second, I had listened really, really hard to the answers: not just to what was said, *but especially to what was not*—because that's where the real fears lay.

Bad salespeople and non-salespeople always seem to think that great financial planning

## I had discovered almost right away that people don't buy the plan, they buy the planner.

salespeople are great talkers. In reality, what we are is world-class questioners, and just about the best listeners on the planet.

The only real skill in this is getting people to open up to us in the first place: to respond to the essential planning questions, which are—as we've seen—basically six variations on two themes:

*What are the things you hope will happen to you and your family financially, over the balance of your lifetime? And what are the things you fear might happen instead?*

And the only way I ever found to get people to open up was to sit there and beam at them, just as hard as I could, the certainty that I was really interested—that I really cared. Because, in fact, I did. *That was my job.*

Caring isn't a skill, or a technique. It's a character trait. And it manifests not when we're telling, much less when we're "selling."

I'm telling you this for the same reason Joan and I are telling you every true, important thing we've chosen to include in this little guide: so that you can understand—and perhaps even remind your advisor partner from time to time, as needed—what the business is really supposed to be about.

Caring isn't a skill, or a technique. It's a character trait. And it manifests not when we're telling, much less when we're "selling." It manifests, if at all, when we're asking deeply empathetic questions, and listening intently to the answers—spoken and unspoken.

# 16

# Stress

# Nick

**"**

I just seem to need to say a quiet word or two here about stress. To wit: there shouldn't be any in your partner's practice.

Hard work, discipline, sacrifice—all the entre-preneurial virtues, as she builds her business: yes. Stress: no. There's a critical, and poten-tially fatal, difference.

Look: ten thousand people a day—three and a half million people a year, 35 million just in the ten years from the day you first read this book—are retiring in this country. After the economic and financial crises of the last few years, their retirement income planning—not to mention their estate plan, *if any*— is in chaos. They have never been so confused, and all their instincts are bad. If they don't find a caring, competent financial planner pretty soon— or if she doesn't find them—they're doomed.

Your partner might need ultimately to find, say, 250 reasonably affluent such families/house-holds—who will be all too grateful to place their financial lives entirely in her hands—in order to go to the top of this profession, and stay there for as long as she cares to.

This is, for people in our profession, heaven's own original target-rich environment. And your partner ain't *ever* gonna run out of prospects.

Once an advisor gets into this mindset, she'll realize that she's not trying to get prospects to choose her. *She's choosing them.* And she oughtn't to be qualifying them on the basis of how much money they have, or how complex their planning needs are. She should be assessing them on the basis of temperament and mutual respect. Does she really want to work with these people, perhaps for decades? Do they seem like the kind of people who will value her work, and introduce her to their peers?

Thus: no crazies, no catastrophists, no second-guessers, no nervous nellies, no rageaholics, no gold bugs, no performance maniacs, no fee-carpers, no debaters, no critics, nobody who makes any kind of veiled reference to Bernie Madoff…no stressors.

The trick isn't learning to fire these people when they've driven her to distraction and she can't stand them anymore. The trick is to see people for who they really are—no matter how much income they might temporarily bring her—and to realize that she won't be able to change them, because people don't change. And, as I'm sure your partner will confirm to you: people tell a financial advisor exactly who they are, in quite vivid detail, in the first twenty minutes of the initial interview—whether they mean to or not.

# Joan

When and if your advisor partner comes home complaining about the same toxic client for the third time, send up a flare.

Why does any advisor put up with the stress of a negative client? Because he doesn't think he can replace him. Why on earth would he think he can't replace any bozo, with any amount of money? Exactly: he's lost faith in his ability to prospect.

And what has crept into the void left by vanishing faith? Of course: fear.

Fear kills.

Even if it means a near-term sacrifice in your income—and it probably will—insist that your partner fire the toxic client. He doesn't need the money; he needs the self-esteem he's going to rediscover when he stands up to this jerk.

Then sit down together, and start the whole process of this book over again. It's the only way.

# 17

# The Retirement Income Planning Bonanza

# Joan

My part of this book has been to put you in very close touch with the tremendous power an advisor's life partner has to affect the progress—and even the outcome—of the advisor's career. I've done that to the best of my ability.

Nick now has a couple of things to tell you about the future of the profession, to which I have nothing to add. So I'm just going to stand aside for a few pages; I'll rejoin you for our summary.

# Nick

**"**

I'm about to hand your partner, however meta-phorically, a prospect file with ten thousand people in it.

Tomorrow morning, I'll hand her another file containing ten thousand new people. I'll do this again the next day. And the next, and the next, and the next. I'll keep doing this for at least the next ten years—or until she tells me to stop, because she can't possibly handle any more clients.

We are speaking here of the fabled baby boomers, ten thousand of whom will be retiring—and clutching all the money they've ever been able to save—every day from here to the horizon. Moreover, as they step into retirement, they will take their retirement savings and make the biggest money mistake of their lives—a mistake that will cause them to run out of money in retirement, and die destitute and dependent on their children and/or the government. This will certainly happen ***unless they are lucky enough to find a financial advisor to prevent it.***

I nominate your advisor partner. And I say that retirement income counseling—prospecting retiring people who are on track to outlive their money, and instead causing their money to outlive them—is the surest and most certain path to the top of this profession for at least the next ten years.

The prospect pool is gigantic: an entire generation, indeed the largest ever. The amount of money that has to move—from the accumulation phase of life to the distribution phase—is literally incalculable. The tragedy of the mistake this generation will make *without your partner's help* is too terrible to contemplate. The amount of good she can do in preventing this tragedy—and the amount of money she can make

**As baby boomers step into retirement, they will take their retirement savings and make the biggest money mistake of their lives.**

doing that good—is without precedent in the history of our profession.

The tragedy, of course, is in this generation's misperception of risk. Having first of all no clear idea of just how very long they're going to live (and need an income), and having all their lives defined "risk" and "safety" solely in terms of principal, they will commit too much if not all of their retirement savings to fixed-income debt securities. They will, in brief, go into three decades of rising living costs with an essentially fixed-income portfolio. And as the path of their inflating cost of living soars above that of their income, they will go into a financial death spiral.

They have vastly overestimated the risk of principal loss, and suicidally underestimated the risk—more accurately, the reality—of the erosion of purchasing power.

This is the greatest single career opportunity a financial planner will ever have. And she just has to know—and tell enough people— four things.

First, the average two-person baby boom retirement is going to be thirty years long. (The key word in that sentence is *average*.) Average retirement age in the U.S. continues to be 62; the joint life expectancy of a non-smoking couple that age—that's expert-speak for "the average age at which the second person will pass"—is 92. I can pretty much guarantee that a 62-year-old couple, sitting down today with your partner to plan their retirement income, can't even imagine this. *And no one can invest successfully for a retirement they cannot imagine.*

Second, retirement income needs are the ultimate moving target. Every year, everything retirees need to buy will cost more. At trendline inflation of about three percent, it will cost almost $2.50 in the thirtieth year of retirement to buy what one dollar bought the first year. If the folks haven't got a plan for increasing their income over time, in some relation to the rate at which their living costs are rising, then by default they have a plan for running out of money.

Third, fixed income securities—of the kind these children of the children of the Great Depression have always thought of as "safe"—by definition never have provided, and never will provide, an income that rises through time at anything remotely like the rate at which the folks' purchasing power is eroding.

But, thank goodness, there's another asset class whose income has always (I repeat: always, over any and every thirty-year period) answered the call. I refer, of course, to the constantly rising dividends of The Great

**Retirement income needs are the ultimate moving target. Every year, everything retirees need to buy will cost more.**

Companies in America and The World. Just for example, from 1935 through 2011, the Consumer Price Index—i.e. the official rate at which our purchasing power has eroded— compounded at three percent. The dividend of the S&P stock index (which has both dividend-paying *and non-dividend-paying* stocks in it) compounded at five and a half percent.

(The value of The Great Companies went up a lot, too. When today's retirees were born in the early 1950s, the S&P 500 Index was about 25. Last time I looked it was 1400. Even thirty years ago—that is, counting back the length of one modern two-person retirement—the Index was less than one tenth of where it is now. But never mind that. Just focus on the key question: where will we find an income that has historically kept pace with, and even outrun, inflation? The answer is dividends.)

The fourth and last thing we need to tell retiring people is that, if they're going to hold portfolios of high-quality companies for thirty years (*or more*), the big risk is that they'll mistake a temporary decline—which happens all the time—for a permanent loss, and panic out of 'em. That's what a financial advisor is for: to keep people from panicking.

That's about it. It's also the one epiphany that carried me to the top. I went out among the multitudes who had set themselves up to outlive their money—in fixed income stuff like money markets, CDs and bonds—and brought them out into the light of The Great Companies, so their money could outlive them.

(When you look at the last section of this book, "Further Resources," you'll find two other books of mine—one that teaches the advisor how to absorb and explain this concept to prospects in rich detail, and one that does the same for the prospect/client, in his own language.)

If I had to start all over as a personal financial advisor today, and could only talk about one thing, this would certainly be it. The career potential embedded in this one idea is simply staggering.

# 18

# YOYO:
The Coming
Golden Age
of Personal
Financial Advice

# Nick

When I was growing up, personal financial planning was something that, by and large, the middle class didn't have to think about very much. That's because the mid-twentieth century was the high water mark of America as a country of big institutions: big companies, big unions and big government. And people's financial lives were pretty much tied into one or more of those institutions.

Your company, union or government employer was going see to your family's cradle-to-the-grave healthcare needs, and would provide a generous fixed-benefit pension (with annual cost of living increases, and then some) when you retired.

**On the day Kodak filed for bankruptcy, the company had twice as many retirees drawing benefits in the United States as it had active employees worldwide.**

Ever wonder why financial literacy wasn't taught in your school? Well, I think it was because the teachers and administrators were both unionized and in some sense government employees. And they just figured that America would always be a culture in which institutions, not individuals, were going to be responsible for the big financial needs in people's lives.

Fast forward to January 19, 2012. On that day, Eastman Kodak—a 130-year-old corporate icon, the employer of generations of workers in Rochester, New York—filed for bankruptcy. Now, Kodak had been struggling for decades, and it never seemed to find a foothold in digital photography. But that had relatively little to do with why it finally had to throw in the towel. The bankruptcy can be explained in one vivid sentence: *on the day Kodak filed, the company had twice as many retirees drawing benefits in the United States* **as it had active employees worldwide.**

It simply could not support the pension and healthcare promises it had made years ago. *No institution can.* And the more aggressively an institution's employees—a city bureaucracy's employees, or a manufacturer's union labor—bargained for rich benefits in bygone days, the sooner those institutions will seek bankruptcy protection in order to get free of those obligations. There are trillions of dollars of unfunded retiree healthcare and pension liabilities in towns, cities, states, companies and unions across this country that will never, because they can never, be paid.

And we may not have seen anything yet. How long can it be before the investor class in America slowly gets means-tested out of their Social Security retirement benefits?

The American household/family just got a wake-up call from the universe. Its message:

## YOYO.

Now, the reference here is not to the ubiquitous spinning string toy of one's childhood. Nor is it a description of how a citizen of the Bensonhurst section of Brooklyn might greet someone twice ("Yo! Yo!").

It is an acronym for the realization that: **You're On Your Own.** The inexorable trend is for the American household to be thrown back upon its own resources—specifically, on its capacity to plan, and on its willingness and ability to practice thrift. This, as we've seen, is something it has never been trained to do.

More and more, if only in desperation, the household/family will come to rely on a personal financial planner. All the trends are positive for our profession, in a way they've never been before. As we said at the beginning of this book: people are all too aware that they can buy (and sell) financial *products* online. But they intuitively know that you can't make—much less ever stick to—a financial *plan* online. For that, they will have to sit looking into the eyes of a financial planner.

And that's why this is—not will be, but already is—the best time ever to be a competent and caring financial advisor.

We've only just begun.

# 19

# What We Have Sought To Say

# Joan

**❝**

We can only hope, as we come to the end
of this little guide, that you have long since
become aware that one essential idea runs
through it. It is that everything that happens
to you and your partner in your shared quest
for his success is a direct result of your own
thought, yours and his.

We hinted at this when we told you that you
had perfect control over how the two of you
chose to process the experience of "no." We

maintained that the only force "no" had—
whether as rejection and pain or as another
victory in your partner's progress toward the
golden "almost"—was the force you elected
to give it in your own minds.

I told you in no uncertain terms (and from
the deepest conviction) that your partner
has a gift, and is surely going to prosper
if he perseveres. But in the next breath I
warned you, as gently as I could, "To doubt
that is to doom it." Do doubt and fear have
that much power? Can they snuff out the
flame of your partner's gift? I assure you
that they do, and that they can—if together
you choose to let them.

I quoted Dr. Hill: *"You cannot afford the
luxury of a single negative thought!"*

I asked you to maintain your faith and trust
that a brilliant plan for your partner's success was being formed, and would inevitably
reveal itself to the two of you, little by little,
in your daily meetings. But I also said that if

you surrendered to doubt and fear when the plan didn't appear on your timetable for it, then it was as good as gone, and would not be coming. That's simply because a plan for success will never be attracted—can in fact

> **A plan for success will never be attracted—can in fact only be repelled—if you're giving off vibrations of fear of failure.**

only be repelled—if you're giving off vibrations of fear of failure.

I asked you—if not in so many words until just this moment—to realize that success and failure are states of mind. You're always attracting situations and outcomes which are consistent with your strongest beliefs and expectations. You can't do otherwise. This is as powerful as any law of physics.

# Nick

There's a school of thought which holds that success and failure are actually projections— that they take place first in your mind, and that you basically just go through life coaching others to validate the judgments about you that you've already made about yourself. I'm still turning that one over in my own mind.

But of one thing I *am* sure, and that is Joan's point that the law of life is attraction. I'm perfectly certain that whatever you and your partner really think is going to happen—or that you just *act as if* you think is going to happen—is in fact going to happen **because you will inevitably draw toward yourselves situations and people which harmonize with your most deeply held thoughts.** In this view, you have a conception of yourself—positive or negative—that's so strong it pulls in people and circumstances that are consistent with that conception.

**I'm perfectly certain that whatever you and your partner really think is going to happen is in fact going to happen.**

With Joan's relentless faith in me, my conception of myself evolved to a point at which I knew I had the power to approach people who I thought might be in danger of outliving their money, and to offer to show them how to cause their money to outlive them. In that way, they could maintain their dignity and independence through a long retirement, and could leave legacies to their children and grandchildren if they chose to do so. I no longer cared what anyone said; I just kept asking. There were simply not

**I knew I had the power to approach people who I thought might be in danger of outliving their money, and to offer to show them how to cause their money to outlive them.**

enough advisors who were focused on this issue at that time. And you know what? ***There still aren't.***

After a number of odd turns in my career path, I developed (in constant consultation with

Joan, and with that other, higher intelligence) a conception of myself as someone who could do even more good by empowering other advisors to carry this message. I might be able to help hundreds of clients directly through my personal counseling, but thousands and even tens of thousands of advisors with my books and newsletter. They, in turn, might help—and I know today that they are helping—hundreds of thousands and even millions of households and families.

Because I was impelled by a genuine desire to help people—and by a self-conception which confirmed that I *could* help—I more or less effortlessly attracted a growing audience for my speaking and writing. I don't have a publisher, don't sell through bookstores or online except for my own website, don't advertise, don't use a speakers' bureau, and in fact have never made an outgoing phone call. (Need I add that I'm currently doing better than ever, precisely because I'm doing more good than ever? No? I didn't think so.)

# Joan

After we put all three of our children through prep school and college without a penny of student loans, I was finally able to start my own entrepreneurial journey. And for ten years, I created and ran the premier salon and day spa in Brooklyn Heights, closing it only when my mother became ill and needed my care in the last three years of her life.

But we had bought the building on Montague Street in which the spa was located, and—with a terrific new tenant in the commercial space, and fine tenants in the nine residential apartments above—that property has continued to increase in value, and has turned into something of a cash cow.

Indeed, with the proceeds of a refinancing of that building, I'm well into the process of renovating a classic Gatsby-era villa out at the east end of Long Island—a jewel of a property that we were able to buy for a song in the depths of the real estate depression of recent years. I'm having the time of my life restoring it to glory.

But I would have you understand clearly that none of this has anything to do with

> **The cause was an idea that two kids in their twenties shared, more than four decades ago. That idea was simply that Nick could succeed as a financial advisor if anyone could.**

money. The money is purely a result, and not a cause. The cause was an idea that two kids in their twenties shared, more than four decades ago. That idea was simply that Nick could succeed as a financial advisor if anyone could, and that I would hold on and do whatever I had to do to see him through to that (in my view, inevitable) success.

# Nick

Joan and I still meet daily, even if it's only over the phone. We still read from a statement of purpose, and a plan if one has already appeared. (If it has not, we do what is before us to do that day, and wait patiently for the plan to appear. It always does.)

We remain open to the suggestions of that higher intelligence which only manifests when we meet in a spirit of harmony and cooperation. And that intelligence still shows up, even after all these years, shooting sparks and amazing us with new ideas. A perfect example: this book had never even been thought of by either of us at Thanksgiving 2011, and it was at the printer by the following Fourth of July. How? You already know how: once we got the idea, and made it our definite major purpose, *we worked on it together just about every day.*

# Joan

None of this would have been possible had we not found and tapped into the power of two minds working together, which are invariably joined in their deliberations by that other intelligence which is exponentially (and, I sometimes think, infinitely) smarter than we are.

This intelligence is, we promise you, standing by and waiting for the two of you to summon it. In this very simple little guide, we have tried to give you the beginnings of an idea as to how to do this. If you follow these suggestions, this force will come rushing to your aid. And when it does, your partner—and you—will be on your way.

We cannot want that for you more than you want it for yourselves. So just let us say: may that day come soon to the two of you.

# 20

# Further Resources

# Joan

I'm already on record: Napoleon Hill's *Think and Grow Rich*, and Aaron Hemsley's basic CD course, "The Psychology of Maximum Sales Performance." They're indispensable, and they're all I've ever felt were needed. They're certainly all I ever needed.

# Nick

**❝**

In that case, it falls to me to mention my own book, ***The Game of Numbers: Professional Prospecting for Financial Advisors***. I've suggested that your advisor partner either already has it or knows where to get it (for the record: **www.nickmurray.com**, click on "Books"). If and when you feel you've internalized everything ***Talking It Over*** has to tell you, the two of you may want to start reading ***TGON*** together.

For a book-length treatment of how advisors

can make a value proposition out of helping people cause their money to outlive them
instead of the other way around, I offer **Behavioral Investment Counseling**. To explain
that value proposition to prospects and clients
—and to persuade them that no one can ever
succeed financially without an advisor—thousands of advisors give away my client book
**Simple Wealth, Inevitable Wealth**. The latter
will also help the two of you formulate your
own lifetime investment strategy, in perfectly
non-technical terms.

I offer six to seven thousand words of aid and
comfort to advisors every month in my newsletter, **Nick Murray Interactive**. And I'll be
happy to make you a gift of one of my books
cited above when you subscribe. You'll also
gain access to the entire eleven-year archive,
now well over 1,100 pages in length. On its
most basic level, I suppose, the newsletter
functions as an ongoing questions-and-
objections-handling workshop. But its real
function is to put steel in the spine (and
language in the mouths) of advisors whose

investment clients are constantly seeking permission to blow themselves up. There's really nothing like it around the advisor community, and I believe it's constantly saving careers, if not lives. You can see a sample issue on my website.

I love my friend Joe Jordan's wonderful book *Living a Life of Significance*, which demands to be read by all advisors and their life partners, and is in a lot of ways complementary to this book. (Indirectly, and without realizing that they were doing so at the time, it was Joe and some of his senior colleagues at MetLife who set this book in motion.) Joe's book is another window into the vital importance of what financial advisors do, but it's much more than that. The spine of the book is Joe's contention—based on the deepest personal experience—that advisors have no moral right to their call reluctance: that their next prospecting call may be the one that averts a human tragedy.

Steven Pressfield's *The War of Art* is a vitally important look at the forces that gather in our own minds to stifle our highest and noblest aspirations, and at how we may (and must) overcome them. Without this book, as I never cease to tell Steve, there would have been no **TGON**.

If Hill, Hemsley, Jordan, Pressfield and the Murrays can't do it for you, I'm just not sure it can ever get done; thus I could easily end this list right here. But I seem to want to add that Joan and I have drawn great strength and inspiration over the years from reading (together, and out loud) the meditations of Marcus Aurelius, the golden sayings of Epictetus, and Emerson's essays "Compensation" and "Self-Reliance."

You alone can do it,

but you cannot do it alone.

—O. Hobart Mowrer